It's the Lord's doing!

God at work in a
North Yorkshire Village

John Mollitt

Kingdom
Publishers

It's the Lord's doing!
Copyright© John Mollitt

ISBN: 978-1-913247-42-3

1st Edition by Kingdom Publishers
Kingdom Publishers
London, UK.
You can purchase copies of this book from any leading bookstore or email
contact@kingdompublishers.co.uk

CONTENTS

INTRODUCTION

Ingleton is a Yorkshire Dales village, located between the market towns of Settle and Kirkby Lonsdale, and located on the borders of North Yorkshire, Cumbria and Lancashire. It is known as the 'land of waterfalls and caves' and is six miles from the iconic Ribblehead Viaduct, on the Settle to Carlisle train line. With a population of just over two thousand, it is a popular holiday destination, especially with walkers and cavers.

Ingleton Evangelical Church came into being in 1972 and, for two years, led a pilgrim existence, meeting in homes and hired rooms, until in 1974, an ex car showroom was purchased for £8,200 and converted into a place of worship. In October 1979, with the building now paid for, I was called to be their first pastor and was privileged to lead a small but godly group of believers.

This group had prayed much for conversions in Ingleton and in the years that followed their prayers were to be abundantly answered. *'He entered a certain village...'* (Luke 10:38) The Jesus who entered Bethany in the days of His flesh by His Spirit entered Ingleton and there were times when we were reduced to being mere bystanders as, in remarkable ways, the Lord displayed His power.

Ted S. was converted at a Harvest Mission, experiencing deep agony of soul, as he was convicted of sin and brought to repentance. Peggy was found of the Lord when she was not seeking Him. In His providence the Lord used a children's meeting to speak to a grandmother.

Ted R. was truly a 'trophy of grace' - the most amazing conversion I ever had the joy of witnessing. With a minimum of human influence, God intervened and Ted, a compulsive gambler, was transformed. Lilian, a retired district nurse, came to faith in

7

later life; rejoicing in what had once been repellent to her. This conversion was indeed an encouragement to those who for several years had faithfully engaged in door-to-door visitation.

Geoff was challenged at his grandmother's funeral - not by what I said but rather by what I did not say. Truly a testimony to the sovereignty of God in salvation, Beatrice, due to a misunderstanding, started to attend the church and, in the mysterious providence of God, it was to lead to her conversion. Alec, preoccupied with work, family, hobbies and interests had a lifetime of neglecting God, but was brought, at last, to 'seek first the Kingdom of God'.(Matthew 6:33)

Five of the seven converts had reached retirement age before they came to faith and this was remarkable, as statistics would suggest conversions among that age group are comparatively rare. But, 'salvation is of the Lord' (Jonah 2:9) and, as a church, we could but say with the Psalmist 'this was the Lord's doing. It is marvellous in our eyes' (Psalm 118:23)

Many churches today are small in numbers, with few conversions, but these stories tell us that we should never lose heart because 'with God all things are possible' (Mark 10:27) We rejoiced with the angels in heaven over sinners who repented and I hope you will too, as you read of God at work in a North Yorkshire village.

CHAPTER 1

TED S
A Distressed Soul

Out of my bondage, sorrow and night
Jesus, I come, Jesus I come
Into Your freedom, gladness and light
Jesus, I come to You

(W.T. Sleeper 1819-1904)

As a farm hand, Ted had gone with his boss to the local village chapel, in Overton, Lancashire. The chapel was in the Morecambe and Heysham Methodist Circuit but closed in the 1960s and is now a house. For over fifty years, Fred Jackson, for whom Ted worked, was the mainstay of the chapel and Ted worshipped with him on a Sunday night. Sadly, some years later the worship of God was to be the last thing on Ted's mind.

Ted now had his own farm but tragically, as a young man, he was to witness the death of his wife in childbirth. Left to manage his farm single-handedly and with a young boy to bring up, life was tough. For twenty -five years, Ted never missed a milking morning or evening for, even when he was ill, animals still had to be tended to. Any faith Ted might have had was shattered and feeling intense anger and bitterness towards God, Ted, in his own words, 'went out and committed every sin in the book'.

Ted was never a 'natural' farmer and was thankful when he was able to take early retirement from the farm and move a few miles into a cottage in the village of Ingleton. He was of a generation, many of whom had little or no choice when it came to employment. I remember a farmer friend who had always wanted to be an engine driver and he used to look with envious eyes as trains sped by at the bottom of his fields. Such an ambition, however, could never be fulfilled as it was just assumed he would succeed his father and take over the family farm.

Consequently, unlike most retired farmers, Ted had no desire to attend the auction marts and he was now able to take up those hobbies for which there had been no time when he was farming. Being a talented artist and a keen walker, he spent hours climbing hills in the north of England, always taking a sketchbook with him. In the evening, he would work on these sketches, resulting in many a Lake District or Yorkshire Dales scene adorning the walls of his house.

Ted was very much inspired by Alfred Wainwright, whose seven pictorial guides to the Lakeland Fells have become the standard reference for walkers. These handwritten and hand-drawn works cover 214 fells, most of which Ted climbed. In his home, he had a map of the Lake District, with the fells he had walked being clearly marked.

In the 1950s my mother had been the organist at Tewitfield Methodist Church, near Carnforth in Lancashire and for her 70th birthday, I asked Ted to paint a picture of the chapel. He was not averse to 'artistic licence' and removed a tree from the banks of the Lancaster canal in order to get a better view of the chapel. In his later years, Ted used his artistic gifts in producing publicity leaflets for the church and in judging the children's colouring competitions.

William and Irene were Ted's neighbours in Ingleton and over the course of time, these humble, faithful believers invited him to Harvest Thanksgiving and Christmas Carol Services at the church. Ted accepted these invitations and later began to worship at the church on Sunday evenings. As he did so, he found his old bitterness and anger beginning to melt away and this was to culminate in a memorable night in September 1984.

Paul Bassett and a team from Melbourne Hall Free Evangelical Church in Leicester were conducting a Harvest Mission and at the concluding meeting, on the Sunday night, Paul preached on the text *'the harvest is passed, the summer is ended and we are not saved'* (Jeremiah 8:20) There was a palpable sense of the Lord's presence as the gospel was preached in the power of the Spirit.

The following Wednesday, I received a phone call from Irene, saying she was concerned about Ted and could I call and see him. As we were speaking Ted's car pulled up outside my house and going to the door, I was met by a man in a most distressed condition. Since the Sunday night, he had not been able to eat or sleep, being overwhelmed by a sense of guilt and shame.

I talked with Ted, and never before or since have I seen anyone under such conviction of sin. Jesus said that the Spirit would *'convict the world of sin and of righteousness and of judgment'* (John 16:8) and I was witnessing a deep searching work of the Spirit. That afternoon, I had the joy of leading Ted to Christ and hours later, in the church prayer meeting, he was testifying to his newfound faith in Christ. The joy we felt as a congregation on earth over this 'sinner who had repented' could only have been surpassed by the joy of the angels in heaven.

So, at the age of seventy-two, Ted was converted and, having been baptised, he was for the next twelve years a most valued member of the church. At Sunday services, bible studies, prayer meetings, open-air meetings, nursing home services, there was never any need to ask 'Where's Ted?' because Ted was always there. No church could have had a more faithful and committed member.

His attendance at the church was exemplary, as was also his service for the church. He became a door steward, welcoming members and visitors to the services. An invaluable ministry, as first impressions are so important and with his warm smile and personality, Ted was tailored-made for the post.

Ted drove a mini car and his vehicle was always at the disposal of the church. He ferried many people to and from the meetings and he provided transport when loved ones wished to visit relatives in hospital. Ted was also annually a 'mobile greengrocer' as he distributed church harvest produce to elderly and needy ones in the village.

Ted was an integral part of the Men's choir, not just, because he had a reasonable singing voice but because of the fun and hilarity, he brought to our practice sessions. We always had a short break during the rehearsals, prompted by Ted saying, "I think it's time we put the kettle on." The 'kettle' never was put on but it was always our cue for a breather. Practices were never quite the same when, for health reasons, he could no longer attend.

Ted had tremendous energy, even in his eighties, still climbing hills in the Lake District and putting his heart and soul into a game of rounders. And, as for the annual church party, we often feared both for his safety and for ours. His tremendous energy was also matched by his tremendous sense of humour.

When my wife telephoned him, she always said, "Hello Ted, this is Ingleton Police Station".

He responded, "Hello Pat, this is Ingleton Fire Station."

However, on one occasion, this banter caught him out. He had been out sketching and unknown to him, the number plate had fallen off his car. That evening, he got a phone call, "Hello, this is Sedbergh Police Station."

To which Ted replied, "Yes, and this is Ingleton Fire Station."

In William and Irene, who had first invited him to the church, Ted had exemplary Christian neighbours. They often took him meals and he went to their home every Sunday night after the evening service. I know that their kindness and godliness was both a blessing and a challenge to Ted. We can never underestimate the impact that our testimony has on others.

His final months were not easy and as his health failed, it became necessary for Ted to go into a nursing home in Settle. For a while, until he became frail and confused, we picked him up for the evening service. As I read the Bible and prayed with him in the nursing home, Ted would grip my hand and say 'yes' and 'amen'. Surely evidence that, *'though the outward man was perishing, the inward man was being renewed day by day'* (2 Corinthians 4:16). He died peacefully in his sleep and though we mourned his passing, we rejoiced that the Lord, who had saved Ted at the age of seventy-two, had now taken him into His immediate presence.

I telephone Paul Bassett to tell him of Ted's passing and he told me that he could still vividly recall the Sunday night of the Harvest Mission. He remembered just where Ted had been sitting in the church and had witnessed the impact the gospel was having upon him. The evangelist faithfully sows the seed and does not always know the outcome but how encouraging when the Lord permits him to see the fruit of his labour.

Ted's funeral service was at the church in Ingleton, where he had come to faith, and he was laid to rest in the village of Overton, near Morecambe. The undertaker took a wrong turn in Overton and cars had to manoeuvre out of a narrow cul-de sac. Understandably, curtains twitched and there were anxious looks as the hearse reversed into the drive of a bungalow. This almost seemed to be appropriate; Ted keeping us amused to the end. Thus, he was buried in the village where, as a young man, he had attended the now long closed Methodist Chapel. Ted had come home.

Pause to Ponder

When he comes, he will prove the world to be in the wrong about sin and righteousness and judgment: (John 16:8)

Conviction of sin varies from person to person but without it, there can be no true conversion. John Bunyan, author of Pilgrim's Progress, experienced a prolonged period of conviction before he found peace in Christ. If, by comparison, Ted's conviction was relatively short, it was deep and almost overwhelming in its intensity.

But what is conviction of sin? In essence, it is to see something of the beauty and holiness of God and to feel the loathsomeness of one's own sin. It is then that Christ becomes precious and His death upon the cross is seen as the sinner's only hope of salvation.

In my own experience, I perhaps knew greater conviction after conversion than I did before conversion. But without some conviction of sin, there can be no true repentance or turning to Christ. We must know conviction before we can know the comfort of salvation.

The Parable of the Workers in the Vineyard

[20]"For the kingdom of heaven is like a landowner who went out early in the morning to hire workers for his vineyard. [2]He agreed to pay them a denarius for the day and sent them into his vineyard.

³"About nine in the morning he went out and saw others standing in the marketplace doing nothing. ⁴He told them, 'You also go and work in my vineyard, and I will pay you whatever is right. ⁵So they went.

"He went out again about noon and about three in the afternoon and did the same thing. ⁶About five in the afternoon he went out and found still others standing around. He asked them, 'Why have you been standing here all day long doing nothing?'

⁷"'Because no one has hired us,' they answered.

"He said to them, 'You also go and work in my vineyard.'

⁸"When evening came, the owner of the vineyard said to his foreman, 'Call the workers and pay them their wages, beginning with the last ones hired and going on to the first.'

⁹"The workers who were hired about five in the afternoon came and each received a denarius. ¹⁰So when those came who were hired first, they expected to receive more. But each one of them also received a denarius. ¹¹When they received it, they began to grumble against the landowner. ¹²'These who were hired last worked only one hour,' they said, 'and you have made them equal to us who have borne the burden of the work and the heat of the day.'

¹³"But he answered one of them, 'I am not being unfair to you, friend. Didn't you agree to work for a denarius? ¹⁴Take your pay and go. I want to give the one who was hired last the same as I gave you.¹⁵Don't I have the right to do what I want with my own money? Or are you envious because I am generous?'

¹⁶"So the last will be first, and the first will be last."

(Matthew 20:1-16)

It is not fair, was the cry of the workers in the vineyard and it is the mantra of many on earth today. But, whilst we rightly fight for fairness and justice on earth, this will not be a consideration in heaven. Salvation is all of God's grace and because none of us will deserve to be in heaven, the number of years we were believers on earth will not be an issue. We will not be jealous or resentful because someone converted late in life is being rewarded in heaven. We will appreciate far more than we do now, that all rewards are down to God's grace and are not based on any longevity of service. Above all, we will marvel and rejoice that we ourselves have found a place in heaven.

I will repay you for the years the locusts have eaten - the great locust and the young locust, the other locusts and the locust swarm - my great army that I sent among you. (Joel 2:25)

Converted at the age of seventy-two, it was amazing what Ted packed into the next twelve years. The Lord gave him an energy and zeal rarely seen in a man of his age and he achieved so much in his few years of Christian discipleship. Ted is, therefore, an encouragement to all who are converted in later life. The Lord can *'restore the years that the locust has eaten'.* However, this does not altogether nullify the regret some have that their best years were not spent for Jesus. It is still far better to trust Him when young and then to spend all your days in the service of a heavenly Master.

CHAPTER 2

PEGGY
Changed Priorities

Years I spent in vanity and pride
Caring not my Lord was crucified
Knowing not it was for me He died
On Calvary.
Mercy there was great and grace was free
Pardon there was multiplied to me
There my burdened soul found liberty
At Calvary

(W.R. Newell 1868-1956)

Ingleton is in a farming area, on the edge of some of Yorkshire's most spectacular scenery but it is a former coal-mining village. The last pit closed in the late 1930s but in 1914, in order to house the influx of mining families, the Model Village began to be constructed. This outer and inner ring of houses, with a village green, was later called the New Village and it was into No.10 that we moved in 1979.

Peggy had moved into the New Village in 1956 and it was to be some eighteen months before we really got to know her. It was the day of the royal wedding of Prince Charles and Princess Diana and in the afternoon, on the green, there was a children's party. Pat helped to provide the food and my contribution was to put my head in the stocks, whilst children threw wet sponges at me. It was all good fun and a great way of getting to know people.

Ingleton Evangelical Church had a thriving children's meeting, *Wednesday Special*, and Peggy was keen for her four grandchildren to attend. When the meeting recommenced in September, after the summer break, Peggy brought her youngsters to Wednesday Special. Most parents or grandparents dropped the children off and picked them up an hour later but, as one of her grandchildren was very young, Peggy stayed for the entire meeting.

Peggy had been christened as a baby, confirmed as a teenager, and, as an occasional church attender, she was anxious for her grandchildren to be instructed in the Christian faith. She very much enjoyed the meetings and over the months, as the Gospel was explained in simple terms to the children, Peggy herself began to think more deeply about spiritual things. As a result, she began to attend church regularly on a Sunday night.

I now see that, of itself, this was due to the goodness and grace of God. Peggy had a son who was a sincere Jehovah Witness and he had sought to involve his mother. Knowing how many 'nominal' Christians have been drawn into the cults, it was the Lord's kindness that Peggy was not similarly deceived. Despite her son's enthusiasm for his religion, Peggy intuitively knew that it was not right.

In July 1984, Billy Graham (the American evangelist) was conducting a crusade at Anfield, the home of Liverpool FC, and some local believers arranged for a coach to go from the Ingleton area. Peggy was eager to attend and on a pleasant summer evening, a full coach made its way to Merseyside. My son, an eleven-year-old football fanatic, had an ulterior motive for going. He wanted a souvenir blade of grass from the Anfield pitch! Peggy went seeking the Saviour and it was an evening that was to change her life.

Dr. Graham was at Anfield for eight nights and on this Tuesday evening, thirty thousand people crowded into the stadium. In total, during the mission, just under a quarter of a million were to hear the evangelist preach. Peggy listened intently, as Billy Graham faithfully preached the fundamentals of the gospel: sin, the cross, repentance, faith, judgment, heaven and hell. At the conclusion of the meeting, as was his custom, Dr. Graham made a public appeal. It was not an emotional appeal but an appeal based on Biblical truth. Peggy was among the first to leave her seat and going forward, she committed her life to Christ.

'If anyone is in Christ, he is a new creature' (2 Corinthians 5:17) and the change in Peggy was immediately noticeable. She had a hunger for the Bible, a desire for fellowship and was most anxious that her family should now experience the inner peace that she had found in Jesus. Peggy was particularly concerned for her husband, as they could not share together that which now was most precious to her. Arthur began to attend church with Peggy and some Sundays, must have gone home with sore ribs, having been elbowed by his 'better half, whenever he showed signs of nodding off. However, Peggy had to be patient because it was to be fifteen years later, before Arthur came to saving faith.

Ingleton Evangelical Church had never had its own baptistry; other churches kindly offering their facilities when we had a baptismal service. This situation was remedied in 1985 when the church designed and built its own baptistry and Peggy was among the first to be baptised, a memorable occasion for both Peggy and the church.

As memorable as the occasion was for Peggy, it was not an easy one, as she had a pathological fear of water. We offered to baptise by effusion (a method of baptism by which water is poured on the head of the person being baptised) but Peggy insisted on total immersion. On the night, she might have had second thoughts, as with this being the first baptism in the church she was rather a guinea pig. The trouble came with the heating of the baptistry and I became aware of this, as soon as I entered into the water. The first few inches were warm and welcoming but underneath the water was so cold that it took my breath away.

I could not give the baptismal candidates any warning and Peggy gasped as she was immersed in the water. Wonderfully, this was not a gasp of fear but was caused by the somewhat icy conditions. Peggy later testified that she had felt no fear but only a deep peace as she obeyed her Lord in baptism. Since Anfield, Peggy had kept in touch with the young lady who had counselled her that night and it was lovely that she was able to come up from Liverpool and be at the service.

Preaching one Sunday morning sermon, I commented we were believers not because we had made a decision or commitment, but because God had chosen us, Christ had died for us, and the Holy Spirit now dwelt within us. After the service, with incredulity in her voice, Peggy asked 'Why me? Why me? She was amazed that the Triune God should ever have chosen, called and saved her.

Peggy was a trained confectioner and her harvest sheaf loaf was always the centrepiece of our church harvest display. As a neighbour, our family often benefitted from 'Aunty Peggy's' culinary skills. When Pat went to Malta for a week, it was Peggy, with scrumptious scones and other delicacies who ensured that myself and the children were not undernourished. At Christmas time, her mince pies and puddings were always a special treat.

Though a skilled baker and an excellent cook, Peggy, for medical reasons was very restricted as to what she could and could not eat. Insomnia was another health issue and Peggy's bedroom light was often on, right into the early hours of the morning. However, physical problems never dampened her indomitable spirit.

Peggy was also a 'Dorcas', being a talented craftworker, producing beading, lacework, tapestry and stitching which was much admired by all who knew her. She never wanted to be 'upfront' preferring if possible, to be in the kitchen: in the words of the hymn-writer, *'content to fill a little space, if Thou be glorified'*. (Anna Laetitia Waring) Such men and women are the backbone of any church.

Peggy had an infectious sense of humour and was one of the most amusing ladies I ever met. Many a 'get together' was enlivened as Peggy recounted amusing encounters and experiences. At the church New Year Eve's Party, with a candle in her hand and a balloon between her legs, Peggy was the life and soul of the party. She knew, however, when to be serious and on paying her a hospital visit, she told me that she was not afraid, just thankful to the Lord, for the inner peace and joy she had experienced since the day of her conversion.

One afternoon, visiting a craft shop in Settle, Peggy was to have a stroke from which she was never to recover. Peggy was a 'home bird' and holidays had been cancelled at short notice because she did not want to be away from home. Being hospitalised, therefore, was for Peggy a distressing experience and it was several weeks before she was discharged to a nursing home in Ingleton.

Although thankful for the excellent care, Peggy, knowing she could not return to her beloved home in the New Village, increasingly longed to be with her Saviour. Mercifully, her stay was short and she soon exchanged a nursing home for a mansion in heaven.

No more death, nor crying, nor sorrow. No more pain, for the former things have passed away (Revelations 21:4)

Pause to Ponder

Jesus Forgives and Heals a Paralytic

²And again He entered Capernaum after some days, and it was heard that He was in the house. ²Immediately many gathered together, so that there was no longer room to receive them, not even near the door. And He preached the word to them. ³Then they came to Him, bringing a paralytic who was carried by four men. ⁴And when they could not come near Him because of the crowd, they uncovered the roof where He was. So when they had broken through, they let down the bed on which the paralytic was lying.

⁵When Jesus saw their faith, He said to the paralytic, "Son, your sins are forgiven you."

⁶And some of the scribes were sitting there and reasoning in their hearts, ⁷ "Why does this Man speak blasphemies like this? Who can forgive sins but God alone?"

⁸But immediately, when Jesus perceived in His spirit that they reasoned thus within themselves, He said to them, "Why do you reason about these things in your hearts? ⁹Which is easier, to say to the paralytic, 'Your sins are forgiven you,' or to say, 'Arise, take up your bed and walk'? ¹⁰But that you may know that the Son of Man has power on earth to forgive sins"—He said to the paralytic, ¹¹ "I say to you, arise, take up your bed, and go to your house." ¹²Immediately he arose, took up the bed, and went out in the presence of them all, so that all were amazed and glorified God, saying, "We never saw anything like this!" (Mark 2:1-12)

The paralytic man was brought to Jesus not because he wanted to be forgiven but because he wanted to be healed. However, Jesus changed his priorities and though he came to be healed, he went away saved and healed. When Peggy first came to church, her first concern was not the saving of her soul but the spiritual well-being of her grandchildren. However, with the passing of time, her priorities were changed and she saw her greatest need was her personal need of salvation.

People come into our churches for many different reasons and with many different motives, but Jesus is able to change their priorities. They might, at first, come for food or friendship but, through the grace of God, they find something much greater—forgiveness of sin, peace with God, an eternal home in heaven.

> [36]*And he who reaps receives wages, and gathers fruit for eternal life, that both he who sows and he who reaps may rejoice together.* [37]*For in this the saying is true: 'One sows and another reaps.'*

(John 4:36-37)

Peggy had attended the church for some considerable time and this meant that, before her visit to Anfield, she was already well acquainted with Biblical truth. And so, on the night of her conversion, Billy Graham reaped the 'seed' that had been faithfully sown by others. It matters not who 'sows' and who 'reaps', we rejoice together, knowing that it is 'God who gives the increase'.

How important it is, therefore, that we do 'sow the seed' when and wherever possible because if there is no 'sowing', there can be no 'reaping'. What we sow today, others may have the joy of reaping, months or even years from now.

Mary and Martha Worship and Serve

> [38]*Now it happened as they went that He entered a certain village; and a certain woman named Martha welcomed Him into her house.* [39]*And she had a sister called Mary, who also sat at Jesus' feet and heard His word.* [40]*But Martha was distracted with much serving and she approached Him and said, "Lord, do You not care that my sister has left me to serve alone? Therefore tell her to help me."*

> [41]*And Jesus answered and said to her, "Martha, Martha, you are worried and troubled about many things.* [42]*But one thing is needed, and Mary has chosen that good part, which will not be taken away from her."* (Luke 10:38-42)

The best of both Mary and Martha was to be seen in Peggy. She was happy and found great fulfilment working in the kitchen but was never distracted by such duties. 'Sitting at Jesus' feet and hearing His word' was more important to Peggy than baking a cake or washing the dishes. May the Lord help us to always have our priorities right.

CHAPTER 3

TED. R.
Divine Intervention

Just as I am! Your love unknown.
Has broken every barrier down:
Now to be yours, yes, yours alone.
O Lamb of God, I come.

(CHARLOTTE ELLIOTT 1789-1871)

Ted was born in Ingleton just before the outbreak of the Second World War. Things were difficult for many families at that time but especially for Ted's, as he was one of six children and his father was a bit too fond of the drink. This meant money was always in short supply. Nevertheless, Ted's was a close-knit family and his mother made sure there was always food on the table. However, there was nothing to spare for luxuries; no holidays, meagre Christmases and hand-me-down clothing.

The family also knew tragedy as one of Ted's sisters died after her nightdress caught fire. His mother, pregnant at the time, gave birth to a severely disabled child and, as there was no real provision for handicapped children, the boy was eventually placed in a home.

Ted hated school and was not averse to playing truant but on leaving in 1954, he got work at Hellifield railway station. In the 1950s, the station had a locomotive depot, a large goods yard and was a major employer. Working irregular hours, in order to get to work, Ted was dependant on hitching lifts with lorry drivers from Ingleton. Though only employed by British Rail for a relatively short time, Ted retained a lifelong interest in the railways.

At the age of eighteen, he was obliged to do national service and much of the next two years was spent in West Africa. Ted experienced severe homesickness but nevertheless, it was an opportunity for him to see the world. On completing his national service, Ted had various jobs before settling down as a truck driver at Ingleton quarry.

Ted married Joan, a Liverpudlian lass who had come to work at the Ingleborough Hotel in Ingleton and together they had four children. Though a hard worker, there was always a shortage of money because Ted, too, had an addiction. It was not drink, for having seen at first hand, the effects of his father's drinking, Ted rarely touched alcohol. No, his addiction was gambling on the horses and this caused him to be in continual debt.

On a Saturday afternoon, it was a regular sight to see Ted going to the telephone box and then returning home to watch the race on the television. As most gamblers know, the only winner is the bookmaker but so strong is the addiction that gamblers themselves find it difficult to break free.

In 1979, we had moved to No.10 New Village, Ingleton and in the providence of God, Ted's mother was our next-door neighbour. One June evening, six months after we had moved, Ted was at his mother's home and Pat engaged in a brief conversation. Ted had no church background but commented, "You must be religious." Pat responded by saying that she was not religious but had a personal faith in the Lord Jesus Christ. Not much more was said but we had introduced ourselves.

We were, therefore, quite unprepared for what was to happen the next evening. At half past six, there was a knock on the door, and there before us was a troubled looking man. "What were you doing to me last night?" Ted asked.

"What do you mean" I said.

He then went on to explain that in the middle of the night, he'd had a strange experience. Jesus had appeared to him and Ted had promised that if the Lord forgave him, he would serve Him for the rest of his days.

I was rather taken aback as a young inexperienced pastor; this was a situation I had never had to face before. We invited Ted in and having explained the gospel to him, we prayed together. I told him the time of our services on the Sunday and arranged to meet with him before the weekend.

Had the Lord appeared to him? Was this a true conversion? What about his gambling addiction? All these questions were racing through my head but on meeting Ted, my mind was considerably eased. It was early days but Ted was eager to know more about Jesus and he testified that his compulsion to bet on the horses had been completely taken away.

Word soon gets around our small community and one disbelieving villager even walked past the church one Sunday morning, just to see Ted entering the building. Church was all 'new' to Ted but he was eager to learn and I was able to supply him with helpful books and literature.

Ted was rightly proud of his *working class* background but I knew from past experience, it is not always easy for such people to be assimilated into predominantly *middle class* churches. They can, for the first time, be rubbing shoulders with professional people who have the kind of cars and houses, they could only ever dream of. In the providence of God, this was not a problem for Ted, as the congregation was made up of 'down to earth' people, with whom he soon felt at ease. He was greatly helped by two older churchwomen who spiritually 'mothered' him and were very kind to his wife and children.

At that time, the church did not have a baptistry and knowing that Pat and I had been baptised in the sea at Morecambe, Ted chose to obey his Saviour in a similar way. We were greatly helped by Christian friends in the town who checked the tidal times and by means of a van, provided us with changing facilities. Pat's parents lived in Morecambe and they helpfully provided lunchtime refreshments, prior to the baptism.

It was a never to be forgotten Saturday when, supported by the church in Ingleton and by believers in Morecambe, Ted passed through the waters of baptism. I was privileged to do the actual baptism, whilst the gospel was preached and leaflets were handed out on the promenade. Shortly afterwards, Ted was received into the membership of the church.

Ted was eager to share his testimony with others and in due course, he accompanied me on door-to-door visitation. It was most helpful to have him with me, for his past history was well known to the village and Ted now stood before them as a living witness to the power of the gospel.

In 1983, the church felt it would be profitable for Ted to spend a week at Capernwray Bible School. Arrangements were made and Ted, no doubt feeling a little apprehensive, went off to be, for a few days, a mature student. He greatly benefitted from both the Bible studies and the fellowship he enjoyed with the other students. One of the lecturers that week was Bible scholar, Professor F.F. Bruce. Only the grace of God could so have transformed Ted that, a boy who hated school and played truant, could enjoy *sitting at the feet* of the learned professor.

In September 1984, during our Harvest Mission, Ted arranged for Paul Bassett to have his lunch with his workmates at the quarry. We gathered in the canteen and as men ate their sandwiches behind The Sun and Daily Mirror, Paul shared his own remarkable testimony. How, as a godless RAF officer, he had been witnessed to by Christian believers in the Heaven and Hell Club in Soho. A stillness and solemnity descended upon us and it was a meeting I will never forget. Some of the men might not have wanted to listen but surely, the Lord was speaking.

Ted's conversion was brought to a wider audience when his story appeared in the Challenge evangelistic newspaper. He was interviewed over the phone by the editor and photographed next to his truck at Ingleton quarry. As a church, we purchased numerous copies of the paper and it was used as we evangelised in the village.

The Spirit of God, which brought Ted to repentance and faith then began to work in members of his family and in a few short years, his wife, sister and three of his children had all been soundly converted. Years later, with profound gratitude Ted was to say, "I dread to think where my family might have been today, had it not been for Jesus". As a church, we rejoiced with Ted and praised God for His saving grace.

Ted's pilgrimage was not an easy one as he faced trials and troubles, which would have tested the faith of many a man. His wife, Joan, died two years after being diagnosed with breast cancer and, in his sixties, Ted was diagnosed with oesophageal cancer. He had major surgery, was gravely ill after two operations and though physically, never the same man again, Ted still made a remarkable recovery.

On being discharged from hospital, Ted was very weak but he shared with me his ambition to be well enough to go out again on door-to-door visitation. This ambition was attained before I retired and on many a Tuesday afternoon, we were out on the doorsteps of Ingleton. Ted never lost his desire to share the gospel with those 'who have not yet my Saviour known'.

My thoughts turned to Job when in July 2011 I received a phone call to say that Ted's only son had died suddenly. More of this in another chapter but Geoff went to bed in apparent robust health but did not wake in the morning. He was only forty-seven and this was a dark providence, no one could ever have anticipated.

Though heartbroken, Ted responded not with any trace of bitterness but with commendable Christian fortitude. He was asked by one of his GPs (possibly a backslidden believer), "do you never ask, why me?"

Ted answered, "No, never why me, but rather, why not me" How true it is that some of the greatest sermons preached have not been from pulpits but from beds of pain and homes of sorrow.

Ted turned eighty on 1st May. Pat and I, having moved away from Ingleton on retirement, travelled over from Burley in Wharfedale to celebrate the day with him. Birthdays were never big occasions for Ted, perhaps because of the poverty he had known as a child. We were so pleased we had made the journey for this was to be his last birthday on earth.

On July 17th, Pat was taking a craft session in Ingleton and prior to returning home, we called on Ted. It was a beautiful, sunny day and we had expected to find him working in his garden. Gardening was Ted's great hobby and he was quite an expert on roses and other plants. However, Ted was not in his garden but sat indoors, as he was feeling nauseous and having stomach pains. Pat asked whether she should make an appointment with the doctor but Ted said, "No, I've had it before, it will pass over".

We chatted for several minutes and before we left, Ted seemed somewhat brighter, especially as he recalled Liverpool Football Club's recent victory in the Champions League Final against Tottenham Hotspur. As a lifelong Liverpool supporter it was gratifying to know Ted had lived to see the renaissance of 'The Reds'.

Two days later, Pat telephoned and Ted's voice was so weak, she insisted on calling for a doctor and this he agreed to. The doctor called, an ambulance was sent for but by the time it arrived, Ted was unconscious in his chair and he passed away before he could be admitted to hospital. The soul of 'a trophy of grace' had been taken by the angels from earth to heaven.

His daughter, Wendy, bravely gave the tribute at his funeral and I preached from John 14 on the believer's sure and certain hope of heaven. It was appropriate that one of the hymns we sang was *The Old Rugged Cross*, as I think this was almost the only hymn Ted knew, when we first met. There were tears in my eyes as we sang:

> *'To that old rugged cross, I will ever be true.*
> *Its shame and reproach gladly bear.*
> *Till He call me someday*
> *To my home faraway*
> *Where His glory forever I'll share.*

(George Bennard 1873-1958)

The interment was at Ingleton cemetery and, before the short service, I was handed a Werther's Original. I thought this was to clear my throat but I then realised that all close friends and family had been given them. This was a poignant gesture, as it was rare to meet Ted, without him handing you a Werther's Original. These sweets were then thrown into the grave instead of the usual soil or posy of flowers. Thus, Ted was buried in the same cemetery as his wife, Joan and son, Geoff, awaiting the resurrection morning.

Pause to Ponder

> [9]*One night the Lord spoke to Paul in a vision: 'Do not be afraid; keep on speaking, do not be silent.* [10]*For I am with you, and no one is going to attack and harm you, because I have many people in this city.'*
> (Acts 18:9-10)

Why was I dubious when told that the Lord had appeared to Ted in a night vision? After all, was this not how He appeared to the Apostle Paul in Corinth? This is not His normal means but I was guilty of restricting the Lord and almost dictating how He has to work. I needed to be taught, *'My thoughts are not your thoughts, nor are your ways My ways'', says the Lord'.* (Isaiah 55:8)

God is sovereign in salvation. We cannot dictate to Him and if He chooses to reveal Himself in ways outside our comfort zones, then we must submit to His wisdom and providence. Jesus said, *'You will know them by their fruits'.* (Matthew 7:16) and the 'fruits of repentance' were so clearly to be seen in Ted.

> *Therefore, if anyone is in Christ, the new creation has come: the old has gone, the new is here!* (2 Corinthians 5:17)

When a converted alcoholic was asked, did Jesus really turn water into wine, his response was, "in my house he turned beer into furniture.". Ted could have said something very similar. When I first called at his house, there were few 'home comforts' but years later, Ted was able to purchase the property; something which, prior to his conversion, would have been quite inconceivable. He then set about decorating and furnishing 10 Burnmoor Crescent and the house became unrecognisable from the one I had first visited. Ted was a 'new creature' and the Lord had turned money wasted on gambling into furniture.

Sadly, there are some who want to be forgiven and to go to heaven, but do not want to change. They want to be the same person that they have always been. This is not possible because true conversion always results in a new person and a changed lifestyle. *'Old things have passed away; all things have become new.'* (Romans 14:4b)

> [31] *'Simon, Simon, Satan has asked to sift all of you as wheat.* [32] *But I have prayed for you, Simon, that your faith may not fail. And when you have turned back, strengthen your brothers.'* (Luke 22:31-32)

Some believers have an easier time that others but for Ted, his pilgrimage was not easy. His wife, Joan, died relatively young and, later, Ted had to do what no father ever expects to have to do, bury his own son. He was also gravely ill with oesophageal cancer and though making a remarkable recovery, he never altogether regained his physical strength.

I remember once being anxious about Ted, as I considered the many temptations and pressures that, as a Christian, he faced each day. Providentially the Scripture text on my calendar that day was Romans 14:4 *'Indeed he will be made to stand, for God is able to make him stand.'* I took this as being a Word from the Lord and it was certainly fulfilled in Ted for despite many trials and sorrows, his faith never failed or faltered. The believer is kept by *'the Power of God through the Prayers of Christ'*.

CHAPTER 4

LILIAN
Unpalatable Truth

The dying thief rejoiced to see
That fountain in his day.
And there have I, though vile as he
Washed all my sins away.

(WILLIAM COWPER 1731-1800)

Door-to-door visitation may not be the church's favoured means of evangelism today and yet it must surely be one of the means by which we fulfil the Great Commission. On arriving in Ingleton, I took to the doors to share the gospel but I also saw it as a bridge building exercise. It was a way of getting to know and to form relationships with people in the village.

It was rare to meet with a hostile reception and most villagers were polite, even if a little wary of this stranger on their doorstep. However, there were exceptions and Lilian was one of them. She was warm, friendly and immediately, inviting me into her home, she was asking about my family and the church.

Lilian was a retired district nurse but since the death of her husband, had also been actively involved in the running of the family business. Though brought up in a congregational church in Southport, Lilian readily admitted that, for many years, she had not been a regular church going. From the outset, it was obvious that she was a highly intelligent woman and she warmly invited me to call again with my wife. This, I promised to do.

31

On my next visit, our conversation was quite theological and it was refreshing to meet someone keen to discuss such issues. Although polite and respectful, Lilian confessed that she had a problem with the sacrificial death of Jesus: finding it rather distasteful that forgiveness could only be obtained through the *shedding of blood*.

Lilian was well versed in the Bible and readily accepted that the Old Testament sacrifices pointing forward to the sacrifice of Jesus upon the cross. Nevertheless, it was something she still considered rather repugnant. The visits continued and with the passing of the months, Pat and I developed a good relationship with her.

Just a few yards from the church, a bungalow came up for sale and though Lilian had not yet attended a service at the church, in the providence of God, this was about to change. She lived in a large house on the outskirts of Ingleton but getting older, wished to move to smaller accommodation, nearer to the centre of the village so she bought it. She also promised that once the move had taken place, she would be attending church services.

Lilian was true to her word, first worshipping on a Sunday morning but soon attending the evening service as well. When I began a new midweek Bible study on Galatians, Lilian was present on the Wednesday night. She continued to attend faithfully and after one study, Lilian was quite animated. "I see it", she said, "I see it. Salvation is through faith in the death of Christ". I visited her the next day and it soon became evident that she now had a saving faith in a living Saviour. Subsequently Lilian requested church membership and in her seventies, she was given the right hand of fellowship.

Her enquiring mind and thirst for truth now came to the fore and whenever I made a pastoral call, she would have a list of things about which she wanted to talk. They might be things she had read in the paper, or heard on the radio but usually they were things that she had heard in sermons. My visits would sometimes last for two to three hours and whilst I found them to be intellectually stimulating, I trust that Lilian found them to be spiritually helpful.

Faith is tested and Lilian's faith was subjected to a severe testing with the death of her only child. Richard lived in Manchester and telephoned his mother every Sunday but when she failed to receive a call, she made enquiries. The sad outcome was that her fifty-three-year-old son had died and no one could be quite sure just when he had passed away. The way in which Lilian responded to this sad providence, was testimony to her faith in Christ.

When I retired, Lilian was still a valued, active member of the church and was always responsible for setting up the communion table. This was entirely appropriate because what had once been distasteful to her, the blood of Christ, was now her hope and joy. Later, as her health deteriorated, it was necessary for her to move from Ingleton to a nursing home near Grange-over-Sands in Cumbria. I shall never forget Lilian and her journey of faith that began with a knock on a door.

Pause to Ponder

You know that I have not hesitated to preach anything that would be helpful to you but have taught you publicly and from house to house. (Acts 20:20)

House-to-house visitation is a means of fulfilling the great commission and a means by which contacts can be made and bridges built. Sadly, few people now 'come' to church and so it is more imperative than ever that we 'go' to them. Such evangelism is not easy and does have its own challenges. During the day, fewer people are at home whilst in the evening people are understandably preoccupied with other things. Nevertheless, whatever the difficulties, we still have the command to 'go' and Lilian's conversion proves that 'door knocking' can still be a fruitful means of evangelism.

Now the Berean Jews were of more noble character than those in Thessalonica, for they received the message with great eagerness and examined the Scriptures every day to see if what Paul said was true. (Acts 17:11)

Lilian had the *Berean* spirit and it was lovely to see. Having an enquiring mind, she always wanted to know what the Scriptures taught and this meant she had a Biblical overview and kept from error. In days when so much false teaching is going out over the internet, it has never been more vital to have the Berean spirit.

May I never boast except in the cross of our Lord Jesus Christ, through which the world has been crucified to me, and I to the world. (Galatians 6:14)

Lilian was brought to see that salvation was in the shed blood of Jesus - nothing more, nothing less, and nothing else. With the Apostle Paul, she came to glory and rejoice in the cross of the Lord Jesus Christ. All believers must do the same, as the atoning death of Christ is the very heart of the Christian faith and the only means of salvation.

CHAPTER 5

GEOFF
Amazing Grace

O how the grace of God amazes me!
It loosed me from my bonds
and set me free.
What made it happen so?
Set me, as now I show
at liberty.

(E.T. SIBOMANA 1910-1975)

Geoff was the son of Ted. R. When I first met him, he was a tearaway teenager, living at home with his parents and three sisters. He was working for a builder, and I found him to be a pleasant young man, except for those times when he'd had too much to drink. One morning, I called on Ted and a window in a door was being repaired, Geoff, in drink, having broken it the previous evening.

As a child, Geoff had occasionally attended Wednesday Special, our children's meeting, but otherwise had no Christian input. Like so many teenagers of his generation, I suspect that God was not in his thoughts. He cannot, however, have failed to notice the radical change that had taken place in his dad. The betting on the horses had stopped and now, every Sunday, Ingleton Evangelical Church was his father's chosen destination.

Geoff was devoted to his grandmother and I would chat with him from time to time when he made frequent visits to see her. She died in 1990, after a short illness and I was asked by the family, to conduct her funeral service. Mrs. R. was an amazing lady, who was a challenge to me in many ways. Her life had not been easy, as she had experienced poverty and tragedy but there was no trace of bitterness, just contentment. Provided she had coal for her fire and food for her table, she did not ask for anything else.

However, there had never been any profession of faith and I had to bear this in mind, when I spoke at her funeral. I paid a warm and sincere tribute to Mrs. R but I made no comment as to whether she had or had not gone to heaven. It is God, not man, who is the judge and so we can say with Abraham, *'Shall not the judge of all the earth do right?' (Genesis18:25)*

The Sunday morning after the funeral, Geoff was present at the morning service. I did not find this too surprising, as in country areas, it is not unusual for family to be present after the funeral of a loved one. What was more surprising was to see Geoff at the evening service. We had a brief chat and I assured him how good it was to see him.

The next Sunday Geoff was present at both services and he continued to be at both services every Sunday. Eventually, after a number of weeks of attending the church, Geoff told me he had been converted and was now a Christian. When I asked him, how this had come about, I was both humbled and thrilled by the answer he gave.

"At my Nanna's funeral service", he said, "I could not help but notice, you did not say that she had gone to heaven; and the thought came to me: if such a good woman as my nanna, has perhaps not gone to heaven, then what hope is there for me." This was the challenge that had come to Geoff and it had caused him to seek the Lord.

Such is the Sovereign grace of God that Geoff had been convicted not by what I had said but rather by what I had not said. Normally, a relative might have been offended that I had failed to say that their loved one was in heaven but such is the grace of God that this omission did not offend Geoff, it rather made him search his own heart. And searching his own heart, it made him see his personal need of the Saviour.

Geoff was baptised and coming into membership, he soon became an asset to the church. Initially, he helped with the older children at Open Door but later spoke in the open air and occasionally, he led the midweek Bible study and prayer meeting. His gifts were recognised by the church and he was unanimously accepted as a deacon.

He married Jean, a local Christian girl and even after fourteen years of marriage, they were still holding hands in church. Their home was often used for deacon's meetings, where Geoff's quiet, thoughtful contributions were always highly valued.

When accessible toilets became a legal requirement, this presented a real challenge to the church. Space was limited and the matter was discussed at numerous deacon's meetings but there seemed to be no acceptable solution. It was then that Geoff came to the rescue. The church owned the house next door and Geoff suggested that the answer might lie in *reclaiming* part of the dining room. This the church eventually did with the existing kitchen becoming the new toilet block and the reclaimed dining room becoming the kitchen. I always see this improvement and extension to the building as a testimony to Geoff's value as a deacon.

Though, by nature, Geoff was rather shy, he nevertheless had an infectious sense of humour. His mother was from Liverpool and he must have inherited her Scouse humour. Many a comedian, who thinks they cannot be funny without resorting to smut and obscenity, would have done well to spend an hour or two with Geoff. He could be very funny and witty, without ever resorting to anything doubtful or even suggestive.

By now, Geoff was working at a school in Kendal, offering residential education and care for boys aged 11-19 diagnosed with Asperger Syndrome and Autistic Spectrum Disorders. It was challenging work but with his caring, sensitive nature, I felt that Geoff had found his true vocation.

Indeed, his growth in grace, his understanding of Christian doctrine and his love for people convinced me that the Lord would open up even more fruitful avenues of service to Geoff in the future. I was, therefore, quite unprepared for the shock I was to receive in 2011, just two years after I had retired from the pastorate.

It was early Tuesday evening when I answered the phone to be told by a distressed Ted, Geoff's dead. The day before, Geoff had set off for Southern Scotland, taking a group from the school on a camping exhibition. That night he chatted to Jean on the phone before retiring to bed. When Geoff did not appear on the Tuesday morning, his tent was entered and it was discovered that he had died in the night. Medical investigations proved inconclusive but it was assumed some heart defect was the cause of death.

Later that week, I was invited to visit Whinfell School where Geoff had worked and I was met by his colleagues, still stunned by recent events. It was obvious the esteem in which Geoff was held and I was able to share with them the difference that Jesus had made to him. The staff at Whinfell had only ever known the 'new' Geoff and were surprised to hear about the 'old' Geoff. I was able also to tell them of the Christian hope that though 'absent from the body', Geoff was now present with the Lord. It was a moving occasion but I trust a useful visit.

His passing was not a huge shock to just the church but to the close knit community of Ingleton and in order to accommodate his funeral, it was necessary to use the local Anglican church. Over three hundred people attended the service and in paying tribute to Geoff, I was able also to preach the gospel.

It was a joy to be able to summarise Geoff's life in four Biblical phrases. Until his late twenties, he was 'without Christ' (Ephesians2:12) but then Geoff had been converted and he was 'in Christ' (2 Corinthians 5:17). For the next twenty years, Geoff had been a faithful ambassador 'for Christ' (2 Corinthians 5:17) and now, though sad, we were rejoicing that Geoff was 'with Christ' (Philemon 1:23).

The service concluded with the singing of Geoff's favourite hymn; a hymn, which to those of us who knew him, said it all.

> And can it be that I should gain
> An interest in the Saviour's blood?
> Died He for me, who caused His pain?
> For me who Him to death pursued?
> Amazing love! How can it be
> That Thou my God shouldst die for me?
> (Charles Wesley)

Not an easy service to take part in but what a joy to speak of Christ, for even the hardened sceptic could not deny the miraculous change which had taken place in Geoff. Indeed, that evening, an unconverted young man called on me, mystified that whilst he was heartbroken at the passing of Geoff, others seemed to be so joyful. Another opportunity to speak of the Christian's 'sure and certain hope'.

Pause to Ponder

⁴But because of his great love for us, God, who is rich in mercy, ⁵made us alive with Christ even when we were dead in transgressions – it is by grace you have been saved. ⁶And God raised us up with Christ and seated us with him in the heavenly realms in Christ Jesus, ⁷in order that in the coming ages he might show the incomparable riches of his grace, expressed in his kindness to us in Christ Jesus. ⁸For it is by grace you have been saved, through faith – and this is not from yourselves, it is the gift of God – ⁹not by works, so that no one can boast. (Ephesians 2:4-9)

I can never think of Geoff's conversion, without marvelling at the grace of God. Saved not by what I said but by what I did not say. This was not man's doing but God's doing and all the praise must be given to Him. No person is ever beyond redemption. In His grace, the Lord can humble and cause anyone to cry to Him for mercy.

For now we see in a mirror dimly but then face to face. Now I know in part, but then I shall know just as I also am known. (1 Corinthians 13:12)

No one can say why Geoff was taken in the prime of life with what could have been years of useful service ahead of him. It is a mystery, the solution to which, on earth, we are not privy. Jesus said to Peter, *'What I am doing, you do not understand now, but you will know after this'.* (John 13:7) As believers, we accept this promise of Jesus. We do not understand in the *now* but in the *after* we shall, *'for now we see in a mirror dimly but then face to face'.* Until the 'now' becomes 'then' we have to *'walk by faith, not by sig*ht' (2 Corinthians 5:7)

18But grow in the grace and knowledge of our Lord and Saviour Jesus Christ. To him be glory both now and for ever! Amen.

(2 Peter 3:18)

What a joy it was to see the Lord at work in Geoff. His understanding of Christian doctrine, his manifesting of the fruit of the Spirit, his faithful service—these were all the marks of a man who, with each passing year, was *'growing in grace and knowledge of our Lord and Saviour Jesus Christ'.* Some believers get converted and then seem to stand still - Geoff did not.

However, such growth and maturity does not just happen. We have to use the means that the Lord has provided: Bible study, prayer, fellowship and personal discipline. Geoff used these means and the result was spiritual growth and maturity.

CHAPTER 6

BEATRICE
Strange Providence

God moves in a mysterious way
His wonders to perform.
He plants His footsteps in the sea
And rides upon the storm.

(WILLIAM COWPER 1731-1800)

Beatrice had been born in Manchester but after marriage, her home was in East Lancashire. For many years, holidays were spent at a caravan park in Ingleton and so in retirement, whilst retaining their home in Haslingden, Beatrice and her husband, Ernest, rented a house in Ingleton.

Ernest suffered from Parkinson's disease and years earlier, as part of his therapy, he had learned the craft of shoe making. His handmade shoes were renowned for their comfort and he built up a 'cottage' industry, selling his shoes from home and annually at the Ingleton Craft Fair. Ernest and Beatrice were also familiar faces in the village on their daily walks with their Pekingese dog, Shiloh.

One of the churchwomen faithfully handed out gospel leaflets in the village and distributed Challenge, an evangelical monthly newspaper, to certain houses. The paper had details of Ingleton Evangelical Church attached to it, and Beatrice's home was one that was '*Challenged*' each month.

One late September afternoon, Beatrice was out, when friends from the Methodist church were distributing harvest produce in the village. This service was preferable to the custom in many rural churches of auctioning the produce. A tin of beans or a pound of carrots would go for an exorbitant price, with the money going to church funds or to a good cause. Thankfully, churches now encourage non- perishable goods to be given for harvest displays and they can then be distributed to foodbanks or to other charitable institutions.

Calling at her house, fruit and flowers were handed to Ernest and when Beatrice arrived home, on being told that the harvest gifts had come from the church, she just assumed it was the Evangelical Church. Consequently, the next Sunday, Beatrice decided to attend the church, in order to express her gratitude for the harvest gifts.

Our harvest thanksgiving services had been a few weeks earlier and so we were somewhat perplexed by what Beatrice was telling us. However, the confusion was soon sorted out and we introduced Beatrice to the woman who distributed the Challenge newspaper. This was to be the start of an enduring friendship.

Having been warmly welcomed, Beatrice began to attend the church regularly and also the Ladies' Meeting. Pat and I made a home visit and soon ascertained that although Beatrice had not been a church attendee for many years, nevertheless, she was interested in spiritual things. Indeed, at that time, she was doing a correspondence course with the Christadelphians, which she had seen advertised in a magazine.

Week by week, Beatrice listened avidly as the Word was preached and it was a joy when she professed conversion and asked to be baptised. Though she had turned seventy and was diabetic, Beatrice wanted to be totally immersed and it was a special night, when she passed through the waters of baptism. Later, she was received into the membership of the church, joyfully accepting the privileges and responsibilities of church membership.

One Friday evening, Beatrice telephoned as her husband was ill and he had asked to speak with me. I called and shared the Christian gospel with him and we had a prayer before I left. The next day, he was taken into hospital but it was still a shock, to hear from Beatrice early on the Sunday morning that Ernest had unexpectedly passed away. Only the Lord knows whether he was saved at the eleventh hour.

Beatrice continued to live In Ingleton, until her health began to fail and she returned to be near her family in East Lancashire. Providentially, a ministerial colleague was now pastor of an evangelical church in Accrington and Beatrice worshipped happily there until she went to be with her Lord. Pat and I were able to attend her funeral service.

'*God moves in a mysterious way. His wonders to perform*'. So wrote William Cowper and it was certainly true in the conversion of Beatrice. Challenge newspaper, harvest gifts and a misunderstanding all being used to bring Beatrice, a dear, gentle soul, to a knowledge of the truth.

Pause to Ponder

Oh, the depth of the riches and wisdom and knowledge of God! How unsearchable are his judgments and how inscrutable his ways! (Roman 11:33)

It is both exciting and humbling to see the Lord at work. Foolishly, we sometimes scheme or imagine how someone might be saved but God then works in ways that we could never have planned or engineered. This ensures that all the praise and glory is given to Him and not to any human being. We are '*workers together with God* ' (2 Corinthians 6:1) but He is the '*author and finisher of our faith*'. (Hebrews 12: 2)

[18]Then Jesus came to them and said, 'All authority in heaven and on earth has been given to me. [19]Therefore go and make disciples of all nations, baptising them in the name of the Father and of the Son and of the Holy Spirit, [20]and teaching them to obey everything I have commanded you. And surely I am with you always, to the very end of the age.' (Matthew 28:18-20)

Beatrice was not converted through reading the Challenge newspaper but the lady who faithfully distributed it each month was 'a link in the chain'. Beatrice came to faith at the Ingleton Evangelical Church. However, would she have ever come to the church had the address not been in the Challenge newspaper?

If we are obedient in sharing the gospel, we can expect the Lord to work, sometimes in ways that we could never imagine. And, share the gospel we must because the cults and false teachers are forever busy and active. Beatrice was being influenced by the *Christadelphians* and she might have become ensnared, had she not been confronted with the true gospel.

> *[1]Wives, in the same way submit yourselves to your own husbands so that, if any of them do not believe the word, they may be won over without words by the behaviour of their wives, [2]when they see the purity and reverence of your lives. (1 Peter 3:1-2)*

Ernest never came to church and showed scant interest in spiritual things, causing Beatrice, at times, to question the effectiveness of her Christian testimony in the home. However, his request to see me was surely evidence that her witness before him had not been in vain. We must never underestimate the influence of a godly wife and mother on her husband and her children.

CHAPTER 7

ALEC
At Last

Today Your gate is open and all who enter in.
Shall find a Father's welcome and pardon for their sin.
No question will be asked us why we so late have come.
Or why we always wandered: this is our Father's home.

(Oswald Allen 1816-1878)

Alec was born in the North East but was evacuated to Ingleton during the war. Such people were known as 'offcomers' but after more than sixty years in the village, he had surely earned the right to be called an 'Ingletonian'. Alec had never doubted the existence of God but readily confessed to me that his *busyness* with other things meant God had always being at the fringe and not at the centre of his life.

Work was rightly important to Alec and for many years, he worked at the Ingleborough Cave. This is a show cave, close to the village of Clapham in North Yorkshire, which was first entered and made accessible in 1837. Expert guides now take thousands of visitors each year through a series of awe-inspiring passages. This is where Alec worked and in retirement, he went back each year to be Father Christmas in the cave.

Having recently visited Santa's Grotto at the cave, with my own grandchildren, I know what a magical treat it is for youngsters. They were enthralled as they were taken by

Santa's Elves through an underground wonderland to receive a present from Father Christmas. These four weekends before Christmas were always a special time for Alec, as well as for hundreds of children.

Alec was also a husband, father and grandfather, knowing the joy but also the sadness that family life can bring. Having married Cathy in 1954, they had five children, three boys and two girls but sadly, his daughters died at the ages of sixteen and four years of age. This was due to a genetic disorder passed on to girls in the family.

Who can even begin to fathom the heartache that Alec and his wife must have experienced? To lose one child is devastating but to have another child with the same syndrome and with no hope of recovery must have caused a stress that most of us cannot imagine. Added to which in the 1960s, there was not the support for such families, which, thankfully, is now available today.

Despite his deep sorrow, Alec was never bitter or angry towards God. Indeed, because of the death of his daughters, he channelled his grief in a positive direction, becoming secretary of the local branch of Mencap. My first meeting with Alec was one Easter time when he arrived at the door with a chocolate egg for our handicapped son, Aaron.

In 1962 Ingleton Community Rural Association came into being in order 'to provide education and facilities for the social welfare of the inhabitants of Ingleton and the neighbourhood. Alec was the first chairman of I.R.C.A. and still president at the time of his death. Many evenings were spent in attending meetings but he was part of a public-spirited generation, happy to make sacrifices in order to serve othersIn his inaugural address of 1961, John F. Kennedy spoke his famous words: 'ask not what your country can do for you, ask what you can do for your country'. That was Alec and the village of Ingleton owes him a great deal of gratitude for his conscientious service to the community.

Alec found fulfilment in work, family and community involvement and yet, something was missing. His very busyness had pushed God out and he was determined to put this right in his retirement. Consequently, he began to attend church not in any spasmodic way but every Sunday morning and evening. His regular seat was on the back row and this was symptomatic of the man, always conducting himself in a quiet and humble manner.

One Sunday, Alec asked to see me and calling at his house, he confessed his personal faith in Jesus Christ and requested church membership. It was a moving service when, some weeks, later he was welcomed as a church member. A joyous occasion for the church and a special occasion for Alec as he openly declared his commitment to Christ.

Alec was a talented artist and used his skills to produce flashcards for Pat, which she used to illustrate children's talks. One November, for my birthday, he surprised me with a painting of Thornton Force: perhaps the finest waterfall on the Ingleton Waterfalls Walk. This painting is now a happy reminder to us of Alec and of the years we spent in Ingleton.

His faith was to shine through when he was diagnosed with terminal cancer and no further treatment was available. No matter how he felt during the week, he was always at church, his wife commenting, "he always bucks up on a Sunday". His last Christmas was spent in hospital, being discharged on the 30th December. Imagine my surprise when at 11.15pm on New Year's Eve, Alec arrived at the Watchnight service. He was pale and weak but this could not break his resolve to end the old year and to start the New Year with God.

One Saturday afternoon, a month later, I was visiting my brother in Wigan when I got word that Alec had been rushed into hospital. I made my way back to Lancaster but by the time I got there, Alec had already passed away. I mourned the death of a dear man who had become a personal friend but rejoiced that having come to know the Lord, in later life, he was now in the presence of his Saviour.

The church was packed for his funeral service, an indication of the respect in which he was held in the village. I was able to speak of his service to the community but also of his faith in Jesus Christ. 'Seek first the kingdom of God', (Matthew 6:33) said Jesus, and after many years, Alec had done just that. He had got his priorities right.

Pause to Ponder

Remember now your Creator in the days of your youth,
Before the difficult days come,
And the years draw near when you say,
"I have no pleasure in them". (Ecclesiastes 12:1)

We are commanded to '*Remember now your Creator in the days of your youth*' because with the passing of the years, it becomes ever harder to do so. Work commitments, family responsibilities, time-consuming hobbies become all-absorbing and the things of God are more and more neglected. Best to come to Christ early but still better to come late, than never at all.

The Parable of the Great Supper

[15]Now when one of those who sat at the table with Him heard these things, he said to Him, "Blessed is he who shall eat bread in the kingdom of God!"

[16]Then He said to him, "A certain man gave a great supper and invited many, [17]and sent his servant at supper time to say to those who were invited, 'Come, for all things are now ready.' [18]But they all with one accord began to make excuses. The first said to him, 'I have bought a piece of ground, and I must go and see it. I ask you to have me excused.' [19]And another said, 'I have bought five yoke of oxen, and I am going to test them. I ask you to have me excused.' [20]Still another said, 'I have married a wife, and therefore I cannot come.' [21]So that servant came and reported these things to his master. Then the master of the house, being angry, said to his servant, 'Go out quickly into the streets and lanes of the city, and bring in here the poor and the maimed and the lame and the blind.' [22]And the servant said, 'Master, it is done as you commanded, and still there is room.' [23]Then the master said to the servant, 'Go out into the highways and hedges, and compel them to come in, that my house

may be filled. ²⁴For I say to you that none of those men who were invited shall taste my supper.' "(Luke 14: 15-24)

Work, business, family prevented those invited from coming to the supper. It was not that they did not want to come; rather they did not have the time to come. For years, this was true of Alec and it is still true of many today, with important things taking priority over the one thing that is of supreme importance; the salvation of the soul.

³⁷All that the Father gives Me will come to Me, and the one who comes to Me I will by no means cast out. (John 6:37)

Such is the grace of God and the love of Christ that, even after years of neglect, the person who comes to Jesus will not be turned away. Irrespective of age, what an incentive this is to repent and to embrace the Saviour. Alec was educated in Kirkby Lonsdale, six miles from Ingleton and this is where Oswald Allen, the hymnwriter (quoted above) was born and educated.

CONCLUSION

We know there is rejoicing in heaven when a sinner repents but there is no greater joy on earth than seeing people come to faith in Jesus. Paul said of the converts in Thessalonica *'You are our glory and joy'* (1 Thess. 2:20) and this was true of those whose stories you have just read. Conversion is the greatest miracle that can occur on earth, likened by Paul to the miracle of creation (2 Cor:4:6) As a church we were privileged to witness these miracles and our rejoicing, though not on the same scale as that expressed in heaven, was nevertheless immense.

At times, pastors can become discouraged and downhearted when, so often, people are indifferent to the gospel and to the claims of Christ. But, when men and women are transformed by the gospel, then the joy and encouragement is such, that setbacks and disappointments are all but forgotten.

Conversions also foster unity amongst believers for without them, churches can become inward looking and problems magnified. When a church is blessed with converts, there is an eagerness to encourage the 'babes in Christ' and not to put any hindrances in their way. This creates a healthy spiritual atmosphere and helps the convert to grow and to mature.

Those whose testimonies I have shared were all humble people and would never have envisaged being mentioned in a book. They were also conscious of their shortcomings and would not, in any way, have wanted me to give the impression that they were 'super Christians'. They were not perfect but were in the process of being perfected. However, they are perfect now for *'We shall be like Him, for we shall see Him as he is'.* (1 John 3:2)

It may not be Charles Wesley's finest hymn and many of the words will sound quaint and archaic to modern ears but as I recall the conversion of Ted S, Peggy, Ted R, Lilian,

Geoff, Beatrice and Alec, they do echo the sentiments of my heart.

Oh the goodness of God
Employing a clod
His tribute of glory to raise
His standard to bear
And with triumph declare
His unsearchable riches of grace

Who, I ask in amaze
Hath begotten me these
And inquire from what quarter they came
My full heart it replies
They are born from the skies
And give glory to God and the Lord

All honour and praise
To the Father of grace
To the Father and Son I return
The business pursue
He hath made me to do
And rejoice that I ever was born

In a rapture of joy
My life I employ
The God of my life to proclaim
'Tis worth living for this
To administer bliss
And salvation in Jesus's name
(Charles Wesley 1707-1788)